Paul Smith

CLIMBING GAMES

Challenge and train your hands, feet, body and brain with over 120 activities.

First published 2009

Published in Great Britain 2009 by Pesda Press
Unit 22, Galeri
Doc Victoria
Caernarfon
Gwynedd
LL55 1SQ

ISBN: 978−1−906095−16−1

Printed and bound in Poland. www.polskabook.pl

Contents

Acknowledgements

I must thank the following people for their contributions, support and advice:

James Thacker, Alan Halewood, David Hooper, Malcolm Creasey, Andy Say, Jon Garside, Rob Stone, Joby Davies, Ashley Jarvis, Robert Lavin, Dr Rebecca Ward, Susie Tarrant, Kirstie Clarke, Sam Clarke, Simon Jacques, Tim Jepson, Giles Stone, Mark Stevenson, Mike Smith, Pete Cook, Guy Jarvis and Dr Adriana Sinclair; Chris Rowlands at DMM; Mark Busby at Big Stone; Lucy Ham at Beyond Hope and Ian Smith at High Places for arranging suitable clothing, shoes and equipment for the photos; past clients of my climbing courses, who had new games and ideas tried out on them; the staff at Pesda Press; Mike Smith, Malcolm 'Bruce' Lee, Tim Jepson and Alan Weightman – a special mention for being major influences at various points in the development of my climbing instructional career.

I should also point out that most of these games have been around in one form or another for a long time. It is impossible to know who thought up a particular game in the first instance and they have become 'shareware'. I would therefore like to thank everyone involved in the development of these games.

Special thanks to Prana, 5.10, DMM, High Places, Bear Rock Indoor Climbing Centre (University of Warwick) and The Ridge Climbing Wall (Wiltshire).

Introduction

This book is for anyone wanting to have fun climbing while developing crucial skills. The games described can be used to work on specific skills or as fun warm-ups; as an aid to a climbing session or as a session in themselves. Climbing movements can be examined and practised in a safe but challenging environment.

If you are new to climbing, you will find games which introduce some essential skills (such as 'crimping' a hold – Chapter 10). If you are an old hand, you will find some great games to help add variety to your weekly club sessions (have you tried 'The Octopus'? – Chapter 6). Playing some of these games can become addictive as your friends and rivals find new ways to play. The overview of skills used in each game will help you turn play into progress.

BMC participation statement

Climbing, hillwalking and mountaineering are activities with a danger of personal injury or death. Participants in these activities should be aware of this, accept these risks and be responsible for their own actions and involvement.

How to use this book

Each chapter of this book deals with a fundamental climbing technique. Some chapters focus on a particular aspect of a climbing session, e.g. the use of foot or handholds, traversing or roped climbing. You can pick and choose activities from each chapter to suit your session and goals.

Each chapter begins with a brief introduction, followed by a list of all the activities within that section along with their learning goals. The games are listed in a random order.

Many of the games develop more than one aspect of climbing. To help you make the most of them, icons appear beside each title to give you information about the possible ways they can be used at a glance.

Problem solving

Aerobic activity

Traversing

Balance

Leading skills

Endurance

Planning ahead

Using handholds

Using footholds

Teamwork

Route memory

Kit know-how

Resting

Body awareness

Core strength

Communication

Roped climbing

Steep ground

Equipment

It goes without saying that you'll need basic climbing equipment such as harnesses, helmets, belay devices and rock shoes. The list below is far from comprehensive but it does include the items required for the majority of the activities. For specific requirements, refer to the game's description.

Balls: Tennis balls are particularly useful, as are a selection of larger soft balls.

Tape: A selection of different types of tape (e.g. coloured insulation or Gaffer tape) are useful for a number of the games. You may have to experiment a little with their adhesive qualities on different textured walls.

String: Thin coloured string.

Balloons

Quickdraws: Not all climbing walls have quickdraws in place, so it is useful to have your own. Additionally, they can be taken apart to provide you with the individual karabiners.

Slings (or even just lengths of tubular tape): A width of around 12–16mm provides a useful compromise between good handling characteristics and durability.

Ropes: It is useful to have a few normal climbing lengths of single-rated 10–11mm rope, as well as a few short sections of rope.

Bolt hangers and bolts: These will give you the flexibility to place the hangers exactly where you want them. However, remember that they will be non-load bearing and therefore cannot be used as part of a climber protection system.

Chalk: Packs of old-fashioned coloured and white blackboard chalk.

Hula hoop: Is there one in your garden shed? If not, these can be bought in a wide range of colours from a toy shop.

Goggles: Cheap goggles from DIY stores can be modified in various ways; the simplest and easiest method is with Gaffer tape.

Pointer: This could be a cheap garden cane, a broom handle or a more expensive extendable device.

Stickers: A range of small coloured stickers and address labels are useful. These are inexpensive and available from most stationary outlets.

Safety issues

When leading a session, you will have to judge the safety of your group, the venue and its other users, and the activity. You may also find yourself bound to particular operating procedures or guidelines at the climbing wall, or depending on who you are working for.

Instead of prescribing safety procedures, here is a series of things to consider. Thinking carefully about each of the following statements will help you to make informed decisions to protect the individuals in your care.

When spotting, it is important to remember that you are not there to catch the climber, but to try to protect them from injury.

Peer spotting

Spotting is a skill that even experienced climbers struggle with; the fluidity of climbing requires the ability to react appropriately to the changing situation.

Does having a person spotting actually lead to any reduction in the likelihood of the climber being injured?

Watch what actually happens when you get a group to spot each other: after a few minutes the spotter can get bored and lose concentration.

The person spotting will tend to be either too far away or too close and be holding the person on the wall.

Bouldering is a good method of warming up and gets the whole group going at the same time.

When a group of novice climbers are bouldering, they very rarely fall off; they either step or jump off when they find it too difficult or get tired.

Spotting can halve the number of bodies climbing on the wall at any one time.

A climber will need to learn spotting at some point, so why not straight away?

Wearing a helmet indoors

Climbing helmets are only designed to take impacts from above.

To be of any use, they need to be correctly fitted to the individual.

Is there a chance of a swinging fall into a wall or arête, or of becoming inverted?

Are you wearing one? If the group is, why not you?

Simply wearing a helmet can make people think that the activity is safe and that they cannot be hurt.

Is there a chance of anything falling from above?

Helmets and their fittings can be a hazard, particularly when descending on an auto-belayer. There have been incidents where the climber has snagged poorly adjusted helmet straps on a juggy hold.

Climbing helmets are designed to protect the crown, but offer very limited protection to the back or side of the head.

Supervising a novice belayer

Common sense dictates that you should be happy with the belaying skills of a person before you start climbing with them or letting them belay others. If you have any doubt, give them appropriate instruction and supervise them carefully. If you are using a new game or activity, the novice climber is likely to be paying more attention to the game rather than the belaying or lowering. Tailing the end of the rope is the most common method for backing up a belayer but relies on the person holding the rope to pay attention.

Note that the 'dead' end of the rope is being managed in order to back up the belayer.

Fundamental skills

Consider climbing in its simplest form, i.e. movement without ropes or safety equipment. What are the skills that may take many years for an individual to discover or develop?

The goal is efficiency. If we are efficient in our movement, we can complete a move or tackle a problem or route without tiring or falling. To be an efficient climber, we need to develop some fundamental skills.

Whether you are a novice who has just completed their first climb or a particularly talented climber who has finally ascended that cutting-edge new route, there are three fundamentals on which we should focus:

- **balance**
- **body awareness**
- **connection points**

Other climbing-related movements spring from these three fundamentals in the form of linked climbing motions such as a rock-over, layback or even off-width crack techniques.

Balance

Maintaining our balance as we move is a basic skill that we have been honing since childhood. However, when presented with new, stressful challenges such as climbing, we tend to forget those lessons learnt so long ago and resort to brute strength and ignorance.

It is often useful to encourage climbers to focus on balance. In most cases, once they are aware of what they should be doing, they will adjust their technique accordingly. For example, once a person is aware that the head is best positioned over the toes when standing up onto a step, they can transfer that thinking to a climbing situation more easily.

A good sense of balance is the key to moving smoothly, efficiently and making difficult climbing moves appear effortless. By being conscious of your centre of gravity when you make a move, you can anticipate the direction of force on a hand- or foothold as you prepare, execute and finish the move.

Balance relies on the core muscles and flexibility. Having good core strength is important for progressing on to steeper overhanging routes and problems.

The key to climbing arêtes is balance.
(Photograph courtesy of Becca Ward).

Body awareness

All coordinated movements require an accurate sense of space, time and force, which can take years to hone. Just how long does it take a child to learn how to walk?

Imagine a shifting and invisible field surrounding your body, reaching to the ends of your limbs during their full range of movement: that is your individual kinesphere. Within this sphere, you will be generally aware of your body's movements without actually seeing those movements. Can you touch your nose with your eyes closed? As you move, your kinesphere changes shape. It has been defined by past experiences of physical movement patterns and will therefore be unique.

When a person tries a new activity or technique, for example when a climber who predominantly climbs slabs tries their first really steep route, they will find that they are required to perform movements outside of their normal kinesphere. They will struggle and become de-motivated. Giving that person particular activities to extend and train their kinesphere and help with these new movements will improve their performance.

Having a good understanding of how your body can move will allow you to link those difficult sequences.

Connection points

A climber must make efficient use of both hand and footholds in order to make progress on a route. There are of course other points of contact that a climber can use e.g. knee bars and off-width jamming techniques, but since these are more specialised, they are not considered here.

There is a strong relation between how the climber is connected to the rock and their ability to balance. Each new method of standing on or holding different types of hold requires the climber to adjust their body position so that they can remain in balance, either while stationary or during a move.

Handholds

A climber needs to think ahead when using or selecting handholds. Not only do they need to have an understanding of how to use that particular type of hold, but also how they will need to position their body to achieve the best possible results in terms of staying in balance. In addition, they need to be able to use that hold in order to move through to the next hold.

Let people experiment with their handholds. Although you may hold in a particular manner, the same method may not work for others.

Footholds

Many experienced climbers often display particularly poor footwork. Correct and precise footwork feels good when you get it right, as it aids efficiency and saves energy.

The art of using any type of foothold is to achieve the maximum amount of surface area contact while having the foot in the best possible position to allow the ankle a full range of movement. Novice climbers often want to try to stand on the balls of their feet or use their instep; however, this makes things harder as it reduces the movement of the ankle.

By encouraging climbers to stand on their big toes, the ankle is allowed a much wider range of movement. This also allows the more powerful leg muscles to do the majority of the work in order to gain height.

Notice how the climber is focusing on placing their foot accurately. By standing on their big toe a full range of movement can be retained.

Warm-up games

It's good practice in all sports to warm up before starting the main session. On the whole, climbers are particularly poor at doing this. It is usually assumed that the walk from the car to the crag is generally sufficient exercise to raise the pulse rate. However, walking from the car to the climbing wall is not.

It has been proven that a progressive warm-up before any activity is useful in preventing injury and can increase efficiency and enhance performance.

When working with groups, you have a duty of care which includes setting a good example by warming the whole group up in an appropriate manner.

The following recommended stages of a warm-up, done correctly, should take approximately ten minutes:

- **raise the pulse – aerobic activity**
- **mobilize the joints – fits in well during light exercise**
- **light exercise**
- **easy stretching – take care as damage can be done by over-stretching**
- **easy climbing or warm-up games**

With young excited groups, a range of warm-up activities can be useful to burn off some energy. It could also mean they are more receptive to the rest of your session.

Some of the activities listed here may not be appropriate for a busy indoor wall or crag as they may take up a lot of space or create extra noise. Is it possible to do the warm-up in a quiet corner or location, where the group are not made to feel self-conscious?

A good tip is not calling it a warm-up; tell a group of any age that they are about to do a warm-up and memories of school PE lessons may start to intrude.

I have included a few of my favourite non-climbing activities that work well with all age groups, as well as climbing-related games.

1
Beans ☀

Get everyone to do different actions as you shout out the names of different types of beans. For example:

- **runner beans – run on the spot**
- **jumping bean – jump around**
- **jelly bean – wobble like jelly**

You could try coffee bean, broad bean, has-bean, frozen bean, full of beans. You and your group's imaginations could really run wild with this.

Variations: The video game, where the group act out appropriate actions to different video controls e.g. play, rewind, pause, fast forward, slow motion, etc.

2
Supermarket sweep ☀

Pretend you are pushing a trolley around a supermarket. Each person copies your moves as you reach for a range of differently sized items from shelves at various heights.

Variations: You could do a gear shop sweep; selecting, trying on and purchasing the equipment that you need for a day's climbing, indoors or out.

3

Scissors, paper, stone 👤 ☀

Show the traditional version of this game, and then get ideas from everyone involved for how to transfer this to the whole body. For example:

- **scissors: do a star jump**
- **paper: stretch as tall as possible**
- **stone: crouch down as small as possible**

Variations: Play as a team game. You will need two markers and a centre line. Split the group into two and get them to jog to their team marker, where they decide as a team to do scissors, paper or stone. They jog back to the centreline and on the count of three, both teams make their shapes. You could play this until a team has won three or five times. Another variation would be that the winning team chases the losing team back to their team marker. If anyone from the losing team is tagged before reaching the marker they join the winning team.

Get the hands and arms moving.

4
Journey to the crag/wall ☀ 🔗

We are going climbing: what do we need? Get people to name an item of equipment that is needed for the trip and then get them to follow you and your actions as you run around your house, shed or garage picking those items up.

Variations: 'Journey around the world' (swimming across seas, climbing and then skiing down mountains, crawling over sand dunes in deserts and fighting your way through jungles)'Journey to the moon' (jogging on the spot, getting faster and faster to escape the earth's atmosphere, floating around in space using big slow movements and acting out changes in gravity); and 'Trip to the zoo' (around the zoo doing impersonations of the different animals on display).

5

Mountain adventure ☼

Everyone involved should perform the actions for putting on a rucksack, walking up steep ground, jumping over streams, crossing boggy ground, failing and having to pull boots out, and crawling up very steep ground.

Variation: Jungle adventure, as above, but climbing up and down trees, forcing your way through tall grass and running away from predators.

6

Equipment relay ☼ ✎

Explain what items of equipment will be used today. Split into teams and have the equipment required for the activity laid out at a set distance away. Everyone involved has to race one at a time to the equipment to select an item and bring it back to the team, when the next person can go. Continue until all the equipment has been correctly distributed.

Variation: If the group has climbed before, also get them to put on the equipment themselves. The winners are the team that is correctly equipped and dressed first.

7
Named parts relay ☀ 🪢

Give the names of different items of equipment, including any individual parts e.g. the leg loops, belay loop, and waist belt of a harness. Have a selection of that equipment spread out a short distance away. When you call out the name of an item of equipment or a part of an item, everyone has to run to the item and touch it. The last person there is out. Everyone still in returns to the start and you continue until there is one person left.

8
Ring-a-round a sling ☀ 👂

Using a 240cm sling (or larger), space everyone around the circumference. Holding on with both hands, choose either the clockwise or anti-clockwise direction and start walking that way. You can increase or decrease the speed of rotation as well as getting the group to change direction, jump, skip, change the height of the sling or any other movement that you can think of, using control words.

9

Group shelter games ☀️🤝👂

Group shelters are pretty much an essential piece of outdoor group kit these days. Being able to employ it as a tool for a warm-up means that it has a dual purpose. You could use the shelter in the same way as 'Ring-a-round a sling' or try getting everyone to flick the shelter up and, by taking a step in and out, form a mushroom in the air. Get people to swap places or move around while the shelter is still inflated.

Teamwork is key to success.

Variation: Give the group a ball. Can they get the ball to rotate around the shelter as they perform a Mexican wave?

10
Human knot
 ?

Have everyone stand in a circle, put their left hands into the middle and hold hands with someone else. Repeat with the other hand, making sure that they grab the hand of a different person this time. The group must untangle themselves without letting go.

11
Endless knot
 ?

Everybody is in a circle holding hands. Pick a person to lead, who has to go over or under the arms of another pair in the circle. The rest of the group has to follow without letting go.

12
Shark attack

Have everybody sitting in a circle facing inwards, either in the middle of the room or a short distance from the wall. When hearing the words 'Shark attack!', they must get off the ground as quickly as possible and then stay on the wall in a stationary position (terrified) until the shark goes away. The last person on the wall loses an arm or a leg.

13

Pass the hula-hoop 👤 🤝 👂 ?

Again, a focus on teamwork but people are also working on their body awareness in relationship to connection points.

With everybody in a circle holding hands, break the circle at one point and have that pair rejoin their hands inside the loop of a hula-hoop. The group now have to pass the hoop around the circle without letting go of each other's hands.

Variations: Have two hula-hoops going in opposite directions, or have them start at opposite sides of the circle and try to get one to catch up with the other. If you don't have a hula-hoop, try using different sized slings instead.

14
Countdown 🫘 👟 z^{zz} ☀

This is a good way to start exploring the wall. Have some markers on the floor about 5m from the wall. Start counting down from ten to zero, when at zero, the climbers have to be off the floor and holding on to the wall. Get the climbers back to the start line and this time, count down from nine. Repeat reducing the amount of time available to get from the starting line to holding on to the wall.

Variations: The climbers have to hang on the wall in control for five seconds. If someone doesn't get to the wall in time, they are out. The climbers have to use different holds each time. The climbers have to stay on the wall with one hand or foot not in contact.

No.1

PERRY

Pinch

KEVIN

Crimp

Sloper

Side Pull

2 Finger Pocket

15
Match the hold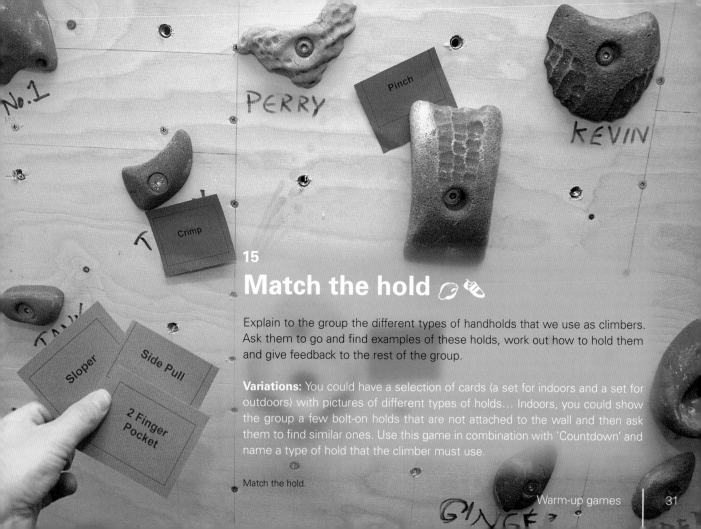

Explain to the group the different types of handholds that we use as climbers. Ask them to go and find examples of these holds, work out how to hold them and give feedback to the rest of the group.

Variations: You could have a selection of cards (a set for indoors and a set for outdoors) with pictures of different types of holds… Indoors, you could show the group a few bolt-on holds that are not attached to the wall and then ask them to find similar ones. Use this game in combination with 'Countdown' and name a type of hold that the climber must use.

Match the hold.

GINGER

16
Which hold is it?

Take a blindfolded group to an area of wall, boulders or base of a crag. Put individuals in different places and get them to explore by feel the section of rock in front of and around them. After a period of time, collect the group and move them around for a few minutes, before getting them to remove their blindfolds. Can they find their section of rock?

Variation: You could do this with individual holds. Get the group to feel them blindfolded; can they find them again with the blindfolds off?

Exploring by touch.

17
Musical holds

The group walk along the bottom of the wall. When you clap your hands, they have to get on the wall with both feet off the ground. When you clap again, they can resume walking. You can vary the time holding on to the wall and walking. This helps them recognise good holds.

Variation: The group traverse along the wall and stop/start at a clap of the hands. This is good for developing a sequence of moves.

18
Stepping stones

Challenge each other in getting from A to B without touching the ground, using the rocks as stepping-stones. Careful spotting may be needed.

Variation: You could play this as a follow-my-leader game.

19
Alphabet shapes

Position people around the bottom of the wall. Give everyone a letter which they have to form with feet off the ground (some letters are harder than others). Get everyone to move to a different place with each new letter so that they are using different holds

20
Simon says

Play the classic children's game. Simon says: use a red hold; stand on one foothold; put both hands on a yellow hold; or stand on the smallest hold that you can find.

Variation: You could play this game on the floor as part of a stretching routine before transferring the game to the wall.

21

The walk-in 🤸 🫚 ☀️

Do you have to take the quickest and most direct route to the day's climbing venue? Use the walk not only as a warm-up but also as an observational tool to assist you in planning for that particular session.

Speed up or slow down the pace, find little rock steps for the group to climb up or down and get them to share the carrying of the group equipment. Can you find somewhere for them to pass those items above or below an obstacle?

Are the group quiet? Is this because they are out of breath or just absorbing the surrounding views? While crossing complex or rough terrain, do the individuals have quiet or noisy footwork? Do they trust their feet, or are they slipping or falling over because of poor balance?

Which option would you choose as the best warm up approach for a day's rock climbing?

Traversing games

Whether you use traversing as the easy climbing stage of a warm-up or as an activity in its own right, it is a wonderful way of focusing attention on the complete range of fundamental climbing skills, such as precise foot placement and fluid body movement. Most importantly, this can be done only a metre or so above the floor.

In a group situation, traversing also allows you to get everyone climbing very quickly, with the minimum amount of equipment. This maximum participation approach can give you breathing space in which to observe before giving individual climbers some feedback.

When traversing with groups, it is useful to specify a boundary above which they cannot use their hands or feet as a control measure.

Feet on the floor

Get people to traverse a section of wall or rock while they keep their feet on the floor a short distance away from the wall. How do they use the holds? Try the activity again, but this time they must have their feet touching the wall itself, while still on the floor. How do they use the holds this time? Is there anything different that they must do? You could introduce the idea of using the inside and outside edges of their feet, not just their toes, as well as the idea of stepping through.

Exploring the link between body
position and handholds.

23

Islands of safety

This is an ideal traversing activity if the steep climbing wall is too difficult for your group's ability. Use slings or hula-hoops to mark islands of safety on the floor. The climber traverses the wall and when they arrive at an island, they are able to step onto it for a rest before continuing the traverse to the next island.

This exercise can be adapted to the needs of individuals. For example, islands can be quickly added or removed, climbers can miss out islands or have the islands placed further apart.

Adapting play to your group's needs.

24

Ball pass

The first climber gets on the wall and is passed a ball. The second climber gets on the wall next to the first climber, who then climbs down, walks around to the other side of the climber passes the ball to the second climber and climbs back up. The ball is then passed to them, and so on.

The ball moves around the wall, but the climbers are only really climbing up and down.

Variations: All of the group are on the wall and have to pass the ball up and down the line as quickly as possible. This could be played as a race against another team.

25

The crossover

Two climbers start from different points and traverse towards each other, just above the ground, with the aim of getting to their partner's starting point without touching the ground or each other. The climbers must climb around each other, not above or below.

The climbers will have to communicate and make decisions about who is to stay stationary, and who is to climb around the other.

26
To the sling and back 🏃

Split the group into two teams and place them at either end of a traverse. Place a sling between them. An individual from each team races to that sling and tries to place it over their shoulder before traversing back to their starting point. If the opposing team member manages to touch them, then the sling is replaced in the centre and no points are scored for either team. If a climber falls off while traversing with the sling, they have to leave the sling where it is and begin again from their starting point. Change the end that each team starts from regularly.

It is worth emphasising that people must climb in a controlled manner. Direct them towards good climbing style and not speed.

27

Parallel lines

Mark on the wall a pair of horizontal parallel lines, preferably in different colours, using chalk, string or rope. Use these lines as a control measure, but also to adjust the difficulty of a traverse for each particular climber. Have the climbers traversing with their hands and feet both between and outside the lines, allowing you to easily adjust the activity for different individuals.

Parallel lines allow you to challenge individuals while keeping the whole group on one task.

28
Dodge ball

Split the group into two teams and have one team traversing a section of the wall. The other team throw blown-up beach balls at their colleagues on the wall from behind a line three or more metres away. The aim of the throwing team is to gain points by hitting the traversing team, and for the traversing team to gain points for each complete traverse that they manage.

Variation: Allow the traversing team to catch the beach balls to gain extra points, or to eliminate throwers. Change the number of balls that the throwers have available.

29
Cat & mouse

This is a fun activity with the option for the group to focus on speed. The climbers will certainly have to move quickly but no doubt they will discover that lots of quick, small, controlled moves will be better than bigger, unstable moves.

Get the group into pairs, one to play the role of cat and the other the mouse. The mouse has to get to the finishing hold on the traverse before the cat catches them.

Variation: You could vary either the starting distance or time between the climbers. You could use a short sling as a tail for the mouse. Do you remember the television series Gladiators? Play this game vertically with belayers.

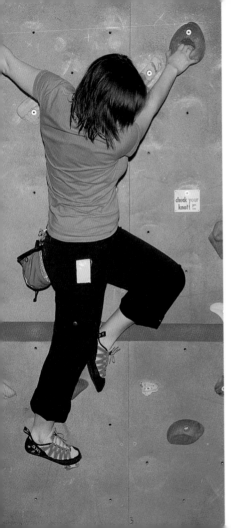

30

Walk like an Egyptian

This is ideal for introducing or practising some of the elements required when climbing on steep ground, without actually using steep ground.

Split the group into pairs. Both climbers get two stickers that are placed on each hip. The idea is that one climber must complete the traverse with their body in profile, i.e. one hip facing the wall, and the other climber must be facing their partner. Are the stickers visible at all times? Try the traverse in both directions and then swap over.

Variation: Climb a vertical problem with one hip facing the wall. Get the climber to traverse sideways like a crab, without crossing hands or feet, with or without matching hand- and footholds. Which method do the climbers find easier?

The white tag is a marker that will allow climbers to coach each other.

31

Limbo

The climbers traverse along a section of wall and make their way under a limbo pole. Each time the climbers finish making their way under the pole, move it down and have them try again. How low can the pole go before the climbers touch it or knock it off? Climbers with better body awareness and balance will do better at this game.

How low can you go?

32

Follow the leader

For this exercise, a 3–4m length of rope attaches two climbers. Along the traverse, preferably more than 10m, there are quickdraws placed at approximately 1–2m intervals.

The first climber climbs past and clips the first two quickdraws, before the second person climbs. There must be at least one quickdraw clipped between them at all times. When the pair get to the end of the traverse, they rest and change positions. They are not allowed to step down onto the floor at any point for a rest.

Variation: The second climber must copy exactly the same movements as the first climber, which would mean that they have to be closer together to see what each other is doing. This exercise works well on freestanding boulders/walls.

33
Karabiner carry

This game is useful for developing climbing endurance and also for reinforcing a skill that may be required when the climber is leading, i.e. finding a good, stable, clipping position. On a long section of traversing wall, hang ten karabiners from a sling or bolt hanger. At the other end of the traverse, place another sling or bolt hanger. Starting from this point, the climber must traverse to the other end, collect one karabiner at a time and return to the starting point to clip the karabiner into the bolt. This works best with a partner who can encourage the climber to complete each lap.

Variations: Use walls of different steepness and of different lengths, or have the karibiners clipped into a length of rope, making the unclipping harder and more like seconding.

Once the climber has got the idea, move on to clipping the karabiners with straight arms.

34

The funnel

Using lines that are not parallel, but closer together at one end than the other, the climber not only has to think about the traverse with their hands and feet inside or outside the lines, but also about their body positioning. If their hands and feet are inside the funnel as it gets narrower, eventually, the climber will fall off. If the climber's hands and feet are outside, then the same thing will happen as the funnel gets wider. The first method favours shorter people and the second taller people.

Variation: This could also be played vertically.

35

Freeze

The whole group is traversing on a wall in the same direction but at different locations. The coach, or a climber, calls 'Freeze!' at random. On this command word, even if they are in the middle of a move, everybody ceases all movement. If they move before the command 'Go!' they are out until the next round. This is a simple activity that works on body positioning, resting and endurance.

Variation: Have the group traversing as above but this time a person on the floor with their back to the climbers is 'on'. When this person on the floor turns round, the climbers must hold their position. If they are seen moving, they are out.

36
Arch runner

Use a section of wall around 6m wide. The climber chooses a starting and a finish point. At the start point, they climb up the wall to about two-thirds of the height and then traverse across, before down-climbing to the finish point. They run back to the start and climb the same circuit again, this time using different holds. Depending on the number of holds on the wall, the aim could be to try to do four or five laps within a set period of time.

Running back to start keeps the pulse and breathing rate high. This can hinder the set-up process for the next lap, forcing the climber to have to think on the move.

37
Two fingers or three?

While completing a traversing problem with a partner, have the non-climbing partner decide the number of fingers that the climber can use for the duration.

This is a useful exercise that helps to build finger strength, important when there are only medium to large holds available, in order to prepare the climber for small holds on more challenging routes.

38
Side-pull only traversing

Traversing a section of wall while using the handholds only as side-pulls will allow the climber to develop good open-hand strength and endurance. It will also mean that they will have to adjust their body position in order to stay balanced.

Variation: Ascend routes using the holds only as side-pulls.

Body positioning needs to change when side-pulls are used.

39

Open-hand traversing

There are effectively three ways to use handholds: open-hand, crimp and pinch. The open-hand method is much less stressful on the joints and tendons, but is the most strenuous as it relies on the muscles in the forearms.

In order to build forearm strength and endurance, the climber traverses back and forth using the open-hand grip on all the holds. If the climber is struggling, they are allowed to use crimps and pinches but must count them. During the next session, they can try to reduce the number of times they use those methods of grip.

Variation: Ascend routes using only the open-hand method for holding on.

An open-hand technique builds
forearm strength and endurance.

Balance games

Activities useful for reminding the climber how the body works with balance. Many can be used away from the climbing environment. Most can be done with the climber's eyes closed to make them harder, especially standing games.

40

Leg lift ✦ ✦

Everyone stands upright on the floor with their legs just over shoulder-width apart. Can they lift one foot off the ground? They need to shift their weight over the foot which remains still. Get them to move their feet even wider apart, to really exaggerate their movements.

Variation: Get the climbers to stand side-on to the wall, with one foot as close to the wall as possible. Can they lift their other foot off the ground? Why not?

41

Stand up sit down ✦

The climbers start by sitting down on a bench or a chair. Can they stand up without using their hands? Can they do this without positioning their head over their feet? Can they stand up from sitting on the floor without using their hands? What happens to the position of the head during this?

As the climber stands up, their body rocks forward and their nose is positioned directly over their toes before they can transfer weight to their feet.

42
Assume the position!

The climbers start by standing in the classic American 'under arrest' position: feet shoulder-width apart, facing a wall with both palms flat against it. Have them lift either foot, as if to try to place it on a higher foothold. What happens?

If they have their hips centred between their feet, it is impossible to lift a foot without some help from their hands. If they wish to lift their foot with confidence, they are going to have to shift their hips so that their weight is over the stationary foot, before lifting the foot they intend to move.

Simple? Yes, but when most climbers are climbing, they do not shift their weight onto the stationary foot before moving the other! The result is that they must 'hang' from their hands while they move their feet. The effort is effectively transferred from the large leg muscles to the smaller arm/shoulder muscles, and this is tiring. It is very common to see this action in novices. This is a small amount of effort, but it adds up with every step.

Notice how the hips move from a neutral position to the foot that is staying on the ground.

43
Step-ups

The climbers place one foot on a convenient step with the other foot still on the ground. Encourage them to explore shifting their centre of gravity over their forward foot, before standing vertically upwards onto the step, as slowly as possible. Repeat with bent and straight legs, and repeat while aiming for a target directly in front, to the left and to the right of their stationary leg. All should feel different.

Variation: Turn the group so that they are side-on to the step and repeat the exercise. Get them to step onto a low hold on a slabby section of wall or rock. Play barefoot, then you can ask them to pick up an object with their toes.

Notice how the climber's nose
is directly over their toes.

44
Swiss balls

A Swiss exercise ball is an excellent tool for developing core strength due to its inherent instability. There are a wide range of exercises available on-line which offer a full body workout. With the aim of increasing balance for climbing, the best starting point would be to have a person to simply sit or kneel on the ball for a period of time. More advanced core strength development could involve playing catch while sitting on a ball. At last: a perfect way of exercising in front of the television!

Who said training had to be hard?

45
Balanced stands 🤸

The climber stands on one foot for around thirty seconds before switching feet. Do they have to do anything to stay in balance? Can they do it with their eyes shut? Can they move their other leg around and still stay in balance?

Variation: Have the climber stand in balance on one leg and then squat before returning to their standing position. Play a game of catch or get them to touch targets arranged around them. Try the same exercises, but have them stand on different surfaces, such as a piece of foam, a small wooden block or a crash mat.

Balance can be practised in a number of ways.

46
Heel to toe

The climber walks slowly heel to toe along a straight line for about 10–15 steps, before reversing back along the same line. They repeat the exercise but with their eyes shut, so that they can focus on what their body is doing. To work on posture as well as balance, they can try this with a paper plate on their head or a bucket of water if outside! Carrying a light weight in one hand at various angles (horizontal arm, at 45 degrees, etc.) will also change the position of their centre of gravity, and they will have to adjust themselves accordingly.

47
Balance beams

Standing and walking on beams or any other stationary object is a superb way of improving your balance in a manner that really resembles climbing. If climbers practise standing on one leg while using the other to maintain balance, they can mimic what they need to do on steeper ground. Ensure that they use their non-dominant leg just as much as their dominant leg.

48

Slack-lining 🤸 🧍

Slack-lining is often cited by climbers as an excellent way of improving balance, which I can't really argue with. However, these skills are limited when climbing rock. How frequently does the rock move when a climber stands on it?

Slack-lining is good for developing core stability, which of course is linked to balance, in a manner comparable to using a Swiss ball. It's also a fun but addictive way to spend time messing around with friends while at the campsite or local park.

Boredom in the campsite is a thing of the past.

49
Flagging

Using just one foothold and one handhold that are vertically aligned, the climber tries to reach as far as possible to either side. Is there a difference in performance, when you get them to keep both feet on the foothold as opposed to just one foot? How far to the right can they reach if their left hand and left foot are using the holds? Are there any differences in reach, comfort and length of time that they are able to hold these positions when using right hand/right foot or right hand/left foot? Why is that?

50
Handless traverse

The climbers traverse a slab back and forth using only their feet. If necessary, they may use their fists to start with, but only for balance; grasping any handholds is not allowed. Can they do it without touching the wall?

Variation: Instead of a traverse, have the climber try to climb a slabby vertical problem without their hands.

A fun way of linking balance, footwork and body positioning.

51

Wobble board

Wobble boards are available in a wide range of different types, from those that only move in one dimension to those that move in three dimensions. They are designed, mainly by surf and skateboard companies, with the aim of developing balance while in the comfort of your own homes. Wobble boards, like Swiss balls, are particularly useful for work on core strength.

52

One-foot climbing

When a climber becomes unbalanced, they will normally compensate with their energy-sapping upper-body strength. By working out how to stay in a balanced position through all the moves, they will be much more energy efficient.

Chose a problem that is below the limit of what the climber is able to do and get them climbing it with both feet. Get them to then repeat the problem but this time only using one foot. The other foot is only allowed to smear and flag. The climber will need to fine-tune their balance to avoid swinging and the need to readjust for the next move. Have them repeat the problem a few more times, before swapping to their other foot.

The task will become easier with every repeat of the ascent as the climber learns to adjust their balance much more appropriately. It's now time to move on to a different problem.

53
Plumb line 🧍 🤸 🤾

A figure-of-eight abseil device (or a few karabiners) is attached to the climber's waist using a piece of cord. The cord needs to be long enough so that the figure-of-eight is about level with their feet. The climber has to traverse the wall but can only move their foot when the plumb line is directly over their other foot.

The use of this weighted line provides an excellent visual reference as to how the climber is shifting their centre of gravity, while performing a series of moves. It will also show if the climber is moving fluidly or not.

Variation: Neither foot is allowed to cross the plumb line.

Where is the climber's centre of gravity acting?

Body awareness games

A person's understanding of body position and awareness of kinesphere have a direct impact on their climbing efficiency. This chapter has a range of activities and games designed to help develop the required awareness.

As the ground gets steeper, you need to conserve as much energy as possible. By climbing with straight arms you are using your legs more to gain the height.

Straight-arm climbing

Climbing with arms straight is a fundamental body position. It allows the body's weight to be supported by the frame as opposed to the muscles. When clipping bolts and placing gear, it is preferable to do so with straight arms. When climbing on overhanging parts of the wall, the arms should also be kept straight as much as possible. The other major body joints (shoulders, back, hips and knees) should be flexing instead.

On the easiest, slabbiest part of the wall demonstrate climbing up with your arms straight. If a hand is touching a hold then ideally the arm must be straight, although it can sometimes be hard to do this. Novices quickly realise that the only way to climb like this is side-on to the wall, pushing with their legs and pivoting on their hand.

Novices should then progress on to more vertical and overhanging sections. As the climbing gets more difficult, it will be harder to keep the arms straight. Returning to slabby walls can therefore help to remind novices about the body positions they are trying to maintain (side-on, hips close in to the wall) and the joints which should be flexing most.

55

Balloons

Inflate a balloon and place it either inside or taped to the outside of the climber's clothing. Have the climbers experiment with the position of the balloons and observe how this additional part of their body affects their positioning on a range of climbs of differing degrees, grade or steepness. This is often a quick and easy method of getting a climber to climb with straight arms and a twisting motion on steeper ground, as they try to keep the balloon away from the wall.

What do you notice about the difference in the climber's body position?

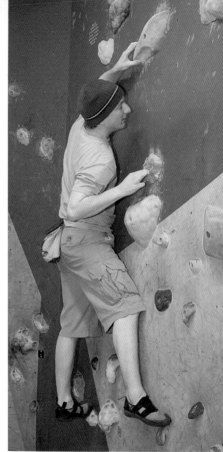

Notice the straight arm and the wide base
of support that the legs are forming.

56
Getting dressed

This works in a similar way to 'one-handed catch' but offers more variety in practice. Hang a range of different items of clothing around the wall. The climbers then have to climb to those clothes and put them on or even take them off without touching the ground, making them think about stable body positions.

57
Musical climbing

The climbers move to the rhythm of the music. Slower, more controlled, movements are required for slower music, while faster music means that they have to move dynamically.

58
One-handed catch

By getting a climber on a wall to catch a soft ball, the climber is required to get themselves into a stable body position. They then have the option to throw the ball back to you or to another climber.

A good stable position will allow the spare hand to be used for something else. Placing gear, perhaps?

59

Octopus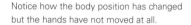

Identify two handholds that are level and approximately shoulder-width apart, as well as a single foothold. While holding the handholds and standing on the foothold, have the climber move their body around and try to touch as many different footholds as possible with their spare foot.

Variations: Use two footholds and one handhold. Have the climber try to touch as many different holds with their spare hand as possible. Reduce the quality/size of either the handholds, footholds or both. Does this make a difference to the number of holds a particular climber can touch?

Notice how the body position has changed but the hands have not moved at all.

60
Hovering hand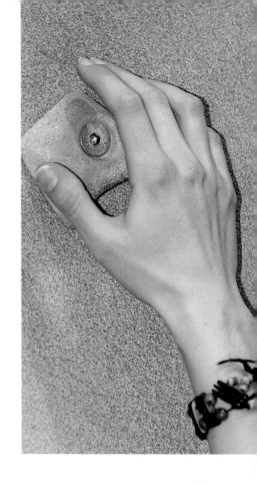

To improve the technique of some climbers, you need to slow them down. They must learn to commit completely to the position for each unique move of a route or problem.

The climber ascends a problem which is easy for them. Just before they touch each of the handholds, they must pause with their hand hovering just over it for a count of five. If the climber is unable to do this without struggling, getting out of balance or pulling too hard with the other hand, have them try it on an even easier problem.

Once they can do it on the easier ground, increase the difficulty. Focus the climber on getting that efficient body position before touching each handhold.

Count to five!

61

Twister

The classic party game can keep a group amused for hours on a climbing wall. Have several climbers positioned on a section of wall with a range of differently coloured holds, well away from each other. Play the game as normal using a standard Twister spinner but have all the climbers moving at the same time. The winner is the climber that stays on the wall for the longest time, without falling or touching another hold.

Variation: Use a pair of dice instead. One should have a colour on each face and the other should be marked with left hand, right hand, both hands, left foot, right foot and both feet.

Climbing Twister is good for developing a stable body position.

62
Hula-hoop

Hang hula-hoops along a traverse or at different places on a boulder problem. The idea is for the climber to reach the hula-hoop and then pass their body through it, without dropping the hoop or falling off, before continuing with the problem.

By passing through a hula-hoop while traversing, balance can be practised.

63

Hip, hip hooray

As the ground gets steeper, going past vertical, the position of the climber's hips becomes a very important link between the hands, body and feet. Changing this position, allows the climber to transfer weight to the feet and still see them, which is important for specific, accurate placement.

The climber traverses a section of wall. When they need to move their feet, have them pull their hips away from the wall. To move their hands, they must bring their hips back in. It might be helpful to have the climber shout 'In!' or 'Out!' as they traverse.

Even although the climber is looking up in the first picture, you can see that she would have a much better view of her feet than in the second picture.

64
The controller

This works best when the climbers are in pairs, either as a climber and a spotter, or as a climber and a belayer. The pair assign each hand and foot with a number, e.g. left hand is 1, right hand is 2, etc. Once the climber is on the first holds of the problem or route, the controller must tell them which limb to move next by calling out its associated number.

Variation: Before the climber starts the problem, the controller must decide the exact sequence that the climber must use. If the climber finds it impossible to use that sequence, can the controller demonstrate?

65
Body circles

This exercise will highlight how a person can change their body position in relation to the use of set holds. Other weaknesses in their performance, particularly flexibility, are also likely to show during this activity.

Four holds are arranged as a square on the wall. Have your climber use just these four holds and have them travel in circles, starting small and gradually making them bigger. Go in both directions. If you were to place a coloured marker on them, would it really travel in a circular motion?

66

Unwrap the sweet

With similar aims to the previous game, this one allows the climber to make a decision between 'locking off' on a hold or trying to establish an efficient body position that will allow them to use the other hand to complete a task.

Place wrapped sweets at various points on a climb. The climber has to climb up to these sweets, take them and unwrap them using just one hand, while still holding on.

If the wrappers are awkward, make a decision on whether or not the climber can use their teeth to assist them. Be aware that by allowing them to use their teeth, not only does the task become easier but you could be encouraging them to develop bad habits for when they are lead climbing in the future.

A sweet treat brings an improvement
in the ability to rest!

Footwork games

Which are stronger: legs or arms? If you watch a novice climber, you will notice that they frequently focus on using just their upper body to complete climbs. By drawing their attention to using their legs and, in particular, their feet, huge advances in performance can be observed. Even experienced climbers benefit from focussing on their footwork.

67
Limits of friction

The climbers experiment with walking up, down and across progressively steeper sections of a slab, until they find the limit of friction for their footwear. The maximum angle that they can achieve will depend on their footwear, the type of rock and their ability to trust their weight to their feet.

Playing with footwear and friction.

68
One touch

While ascending a problem, the climber is only allowed to use the first foothold that they touch instead of feeling around lots of different holds. This should also get them to climb in a less frantic manner.

Variation: Use this activity with both hands and feet, or just hands.

69
Sticky feet

In this game, once a foot is placed on a hold, the climber is not allowed to adjust its position. This will force the climber to not only think about how they are going to use the hold with their foot but it will also get them to slow down and watch themselves place that foot accurately.

70
Giant steps, ant steps

The climber has to ascend the route or problem twice. During the first ascent, they have to make the biggest steps possible. During the second ascent, they have to make as many small steps as possible. Can they beat the number of steps their belayer manages?

71

Watch your feet

Accuracy regarding foot placement is very important. From the moment that they decide to move a foot, the climber fixes their gaze on it until it is in the correct useable position on the next foothold.

Variation: As a foot is just 1cm above a new hold, the climber must count out loud to three before placing it.

Checking that the foot is placed exactly where it is required. (Photograph courtesy of Simon Jacques).

72

Corks

This is similar to the Fontainebleau classic training method of placing small coins on the footholds of a problem which have not to be disturbed. Due to the nature of most climbing walls (the holds tend to be quite large), we are going to use corks. With the corks placed on the footholds of a traverse, the climbers take it in turns to try to complete the traverse while knocking off the least number of corks.

Variation: Try this on a vertical boulder problem but be aware of falling corks. Try small coins.

The foot must be placed with care so that the cork is not knocked off the foothold.

73

Which smear to use?

On a slab climb, ask the climbers to examine closely the surface of the rock, not only with their eyes but also with their hands. They are looking for the different changes in angle, as well as any other irregularity, that they may be able to use as a foothold or smear. They can mark potential footholds with tape and then try them out. Make sure that any marks made are removed afterwards.

74

Secret agent

Precise footwork is a fundamental climbing skill. This easy and highly effective game develops this. It is also the quietest game in this book!

The climbers have to climb making no noise, especially with their feet and hands. Demonstrate climbing very slowly and precisely as you creep up on your prey making as little noise as possible. Then watch everyone climbing more precisely than a Stanage veteran!

75
Red for right foot

Mark some of the footholds with a bit of red tape or a red dot. The climber can only use their right foot on those holds. Either foot can use the unmarked holds.

Variation: Use another colour for the left foot. The climbers decide on which foothold is going to used by which foot before they start climbing and mark their own holds. Do they need to be adjusted after an initial attempt at the problem?

By having the climber mark the footholds that they are going to use, it starts them thinking about their sequence.

The one-armed climber 🤸 🧗

The climbers ascend a route using both hands. They then do the same route with their non-dominant hand behind their back or down by their side. Have them focus on placing all of their weight on their feet and tell them that they can only use their hand purely for balance. Now they repeat the climb but this time using only the non-dominant hand to assist them. Is there a difference in their climbing style? What feels different for them?

By only using one arm, the climber has think carefully about how they are going to adjust their body and place their feet.

77

Limited use of hands 🎾 🧗

To encourage climbers to use their feet more, force them to use their hands less. Give them a tennis ball to hold in each hand, place a stone on the back of each hand, make fists with their thumb inside or even get them to place their hands on their hips.

Do you know a climber that just pulls with their arms? Have them climb with a tennis ball in each hand, to force them to use their feet.

78

Features for hands

The climber can use any holds or features for their feet but they must only use the textured features on the wall for their hands. This is a useful way of limiting the amount of upper body strength that the climber can use.

79

Copycat

Climb the same problem as someone else, focusing on using the same footholds as they did.

Variation: Copy their whole sequence.

80

Push

Each time the climber places their foot they need to shout 'Push!' as a reminder to apply pressure downwards onto the hold. This also encourages them to use their leg muscles instead of pulling with their arms.

81

Inside, outside, heel, toe

This is useful as it makes the climber more aware of the parts of the foot that they are using while climbing.

With novices, show the climber what you mean by each of these words regarding foot placement.

The climber then ascends a route or problem, calling out the part of the foot they are using.

Variations: The belayer or spotter calls out which part of the foot the climber has to use on the next foothold. Ascend the same problem several times, each time using your foot in only one position.

82

Swivelling

The climber swaps their feet on every single foothold that they use, using the inside and outside edges of their shoes. This is not only good for preparing someone to climb steeper ground but hopefully it will make them realise that there is a link between their upper body and their feet.

By taping over the top half of a pair of goggles, the climber can only see holds that are below them.

83

Eyes down

Complete a problem without looking down at all, and then repeat the problem without looking up. Which is easier to do? Why?

Does the climber know what they are doing? Ask them how often they think they look down then film them on a problem. Show them the film to see if they are correct about their idea of what they are actually doing.

Variation: Use cheap safety goggles that have had sections taped over so that you can only look up or down or only see through thin slits. This forces the climber to focus on the holds that they wish to use. It also allows the coach to work out what they are really looking at when they complete a move.

84

Weighting the feet 🪳 🏃

While using good handholds, the climber puts their feet on what they regard as poor footholds. They will need to relax the amount of arm and finger power that they are using and gradually increase the weight being transferred through their feet. Can they completely let go with one hand? Try this exercise on a range of different angled and textured surfaces, with increasingly poor footholds.

Variation: After completing a problem, either have someone change the footholds or use a different set of holds, ensuring that they are poorer footholds. Repeat the problem. As the difficulty of the climb increases, the footholds often become much less positive.

85

Hands down

Limiting the distance that the climber can reach prevents overstretching and forces them to find more appropriate intermediate footholds in order to gain height. Use body parts as reference points (head, shoulders, chest, etc.) and have them climb without their hands going up past them.

Variation: Get the climber to imagine that there is a box drawn in front of their head and that they are only allowed to use handholds within their box. Change the size of the box.

By keeping their hands low, the climber is not over-reaching and can therefore maintain their centre of gravity over their toes. (Photograph courtesy of Simon Jacques).

86
Double-step, then reach 🥕 🏃

Novice climbers tend to look for a handhold, make the move by pulling with their arms and finally decide to move their feet afterwards, without any real thought. The much preferred, and more energy-efficient, method is to identify the next handhold, move the feet up before pushing with the legs and then finally touch that handhold.

Have the climber choose their next handhold but not reach for it. They will then need to step up both of their feet, while minimising the amount that they are pulling on their current handhold. When both feet have been moved up, the climber is then free to reach for the handhold. Have them repeat this for the rest of the climb and even the rest of that climbing session. If they are getting confused, have them say 'Step, step' with each foot movement and 'Reach, reach' as their hands are moved.

Step up, stand up and then reach.

87

Down-climb

The climber ascends a route or boulder problem and then tries to down-climb it, i.e. descend the route using exactly the same holds, while staying in control. This forces them to look more carefully at their foot placements and body positioning.

88

Inside and outside

The climber ascends the same problem three times. The first time, they must climb the problem face-on and with just their toes. The second time, have them climb with their whole body facing left. This forces them to use the inside edge of their left foot and the outside edge of their right foot. The third and final time, they climb facing right, using the inside edge of their right foot and the outside edge of their left foot.

Ensure that the climber is pushing with their back foot and pulling towards the next hold with their forward foot.

89

What is under your pit?

The climbers hold a tennis ball, a balloon or small beanbag under each armpit while they try to complete a problem or a traverse. This will make them climb with their arms close to their body, limiting their reach and therefore forcing them to use their feet more effectively.

90

Taps

This is a quick method of focusing a climber's attention on how they could be using their feet more effectively. Every time the climber uses any hand to help them ascend a problem, they must tap themselves on the head and count the taps. Can they reduce the number of times that they use their hands?

Un-roped games

A range of activities that are hard to categorise apart from the fact that they don't necessarily require the use of ropes. They are therefore suited for use on a bouldering wall.

Add on (version 1)

Known by the majority of indoor wall users, this game is best played with a small group of climbers of a similar ability. 'Add on' is great for training endurance and memory.

One person begins by choosing the starting handholds and just pulls on them. The next person uses the same starting holds and adds on another move. The third person then starts from the beginning and adds on another move of their own, and so on. The game continues until someone makes a mistake, at which point they are out.

Variations: The climbers have to use the same hand and footholds. When a climber fails to do a move, they lose one of three lives. Once a sequence has been set, can holds be missed out?

92
Add on (version 2)

With this version, each climber adds 5–8 moves each time. The second person copies the first person's starting moves, and then adds on 5–8 of their own. The third person copies the second person's moves and adds on 5–8 moves of their own, and so the problem continues.

Each of these moves is likely to be harder than during a normal game of 'add on', and with this version, the climbers are doing more moves only once and are therefore working on their on-sighting skills.

You can increase the number of moves that are added each time but since people will struggle to follow all of the moves at first, it's best to build up gradually.

Variation: Have a bag of balls, with different numbers on them ranging from 1 to 10. Before a climber ascends the problem, they have to draw a ball from the bag and add on that number of moves.

93

Elimination

This works really well with the game 'add on'. Once the problem has been finished, whoever completed the problem first gets to eliminate one handhold. The rest of the group have to complete the new problem. Whoever manages this can then eliminate another hold, and so on.

Variation: Find a problem that the whole of a small group of climbers can do. The first climber chooses which hold to eliminate and has three chances to do so. If they fail to complete the problem, they lose one of their three lives and it becomes the turn of the next climber. The game continues until there is only one climber left or no holds to eliminate.

94

Climbing-wall golf

As a group, the climbers choose a start and finish hold and then take turns trying to link the holds together in the minimum number of moves.

Variations: Get the climbers to say how many handholds that they think they need to use to link the starting and finishing holds. For example, if climber A thinks 6 holds but climber B thinks 5 holds, climber A challenges climber B to do it using 5 holds. Climber B wins if they do it, Climber A wins if they don't. To stop people overreaching for holds, you could have them touch the next hold that they are going to use with their elbow first.

95

Take away

This is a game that gets progressively harder. Using a defined section of wall as well as a starting and finishing hold, a climber moves from the start to the finish using whichever holds they wish. Once those holds have been used, no-one else can use them (put tape them over them, put a small cross next to them or just remember). The next climber then needs to get from the start hold to the finishing hold using any of the remaining holds.

Variation: Everyone repeats the problem once before everyone joins in a group decision about which holds are to be removed.

If your memory is not up it, tape over the holds that have been used.

96
Problem evolution

This can be a useful activity for two climbers of a similar ability, even if they have completely different styles or climbing preferences.

The pair of climbers chose a start and a finish hold, which remain constant throughout the activity. The first climber makes seven different moves to get to the finishing hold. The second climber then repeats the problem. After changing two or three of the moves, the second climber completes the problem again. The first climber then repeats this new problem, changes two or three of the moves and then climbs it again.

These rotations should continue, for example for a dozen times, with each rotation making the problem different so that a completely new problem evolves.

97

Can you remember?

Working in pairs, the first person points out a sequence of four moves. The second person then has to climb this problem without additional information or having the holds shown to them again.

The person that set the problem counts the number of moves that the climber correctly remembered. It may be useful to use a video camera here so that there are no disagreements. When climbers are consistently getting the sequence of four moves correct, increase the number of moves in the sequence.

Variation: Have the person setting the sequence climb the problem first, which will make the second climber have to think about their observational position. Can they see all the moves?

The pointer (version 1) 🏁 🏃

This activity works best in pairs with one climber and one pointer equipped with a broom handle or extendable pole. The climber gets onto the wall and the pointer points out the next handhold where the climber has to move. The two key points here are A, the timing of the pointer, so that the climber is not left hanging around for too long, and B, to ensure that the pointer doesn't make things too difficult for the climber. The aim is to challenge the climber, not to give them moves that are too hard or outrageous.

The aim for both the climber and the person doing the pointing is for the climber to stay on the wall for as long as possible. If you get the speed correct, this will really work the climber's decision-making skills and hence, their on-sighting ability.

Variation: Point out footholds as well as handholds. Once you have pointed out the next hold, tell the climber which hand they have to use.

Pointing out the next hold in the sequence to the climber.

The pointer (version 2) 🤸 ☀ 🏳 🏃

This esercise is better at working endurance than version 1 but also helps with building balance in a similar manner to 'one-foot climbing'. Choose a starting and finishing hold on a traverse that requires around twenty moves in order to link them.

The person who is going to take charge of the pointer is responsible for identifying the holds that the climber has to use with their right hand. The climber is then free to choose whichever holds they wish for their left hand. Once one lap has been completed, start again. This time, the person who is pointing identifies the holds for the climber's left hand and the climber is free to choose their own holds for their right hand. Do at least four laps before changing over, using different sections of wall or even doing the same section in reverse.

Note that the pointer should choose a mixture of moves to both large and small holds, or even awkward moves. Remember that in order for this to provide an endurance exercise, the moves need to be within the capabilities of the climber but should still push them.

100

Straight-leg climbing 🪨 🤸

When climbing, generally we should try to use our leg muscles as much as we possibly can, thus allowing some of the stronger muscles in the body to do most of the work.

While climbing a vertical problem, the climber must stand on a foothold and straighten their leg fully to the satisfaction of their partner before being allowed to put their other foot on the next foothold. This is continued to the top.

Have the climber straighten their leg
before moving their other foot.

101

Resting

Having the ability to rest while climbing may mean the difference between success or failure on that problem or route.

While bouldering on big holds, encourage the climber to find two or three resting holds for each hand. When they touch one of them, they have to rest. By making sure that their weight is over their feet as much as possible, by dropping an arm and looking at the ground they can open up the shoulders and hence promote blood flow into the lower arm. Have them close their eyes and breathe deeply. To reinforce the process have the climber say the words 'Breathe' or 'Rest'.

Have the climber climb for as long a period of time as possible, resting as much as they can, by timing the exercise or counting the number of laps that they do. This provides an excellent measure of their progress.

102
Look at
the holds

Getting a group to search for small objects or sweets hidden around a bouldering wall is an interesting way to encourage them to look at different types of holds. This is particularly effective if you get them to describe where they found their object or sweet.

103
Rest on every move

How often do you a see a climber moving quickly up a problem, then falling just one or two moves from the top? Fairly frequently? It is very common, and happens because the climber is rushing the problem as they feel that they don't have enough stamina to complete it in one go. What they need to do is learn to rest.

Set the climber on a problem that is relatively easy for them. Every time they move their hand, they must adjust their body position so that they remain in balance, look at the ground and take three deep breaths. Continue like this for the whole problem.

Note that some climbers may still get to the top of the problem and complain that they feel tired, even with all of the resting. This is most likely because of over-gripping with the hands or not getting into proper resting positions. The climber must really master this activity on the easier ground before increasing the difficulty.

104

Fixed time on the wall

Set a timer for between 10–20 minutes. Start it when the climber gets onto the wall, telling them they can't get off until the time is up. While they are on the wall, they have to move around and try moves of different degrees of difficultly as well as resting. This would be the prefect opportunity to practise resting skills.

Variation: Get a climber who is 'pumped' from just completing a route straight onto the bouldering wall, where they must remain off the ground for 10 minutes on a large hold or pair of holds. While in position, they will need to shake out each arm, rest, relax and stretch their forearms. By the time they come off the wall, they should no longer be pumped. This will help the climber realise that they are able to recover, even when on a route.

105

Too tight, too loose

Try this one after everyone is warmed-up to reduce the chance of injury.

Show your climbers how the holds can be held too tightly. Get them try a short problem while trying to hold the holds as tightly as they can. What do they notice? Next, have them climb the same problem holding the holds as lightly as they possibly can. What do they notice this time and what do they have to do differently?

You'll hopefully get the response that they are becoming 'pumped' i.e. are losing power and strength during the first attempt. The second time, they should find that they have to change their body position.

106

Bad holds

The climbers set themselves a 25–30 move problem, which is just below their on-sight ability. They climb it once and then replace the three best holds from the problem with three new close-by holds, making them the three worst but usable holds on the problem. They then climb the problem again, replacing the current three best holds. Continue like this until the climbers fall, or the problem becomes too difficult. Either allow them to work the problem or move to different section of wall.

Variation: Start below a pair of climbers' on-sight ability. Have them complete the same exercise as above, taking it in turns to decide which are the best holds to remove.

107

Home base

Pick a good starting hold which is not only good enough to both rest and recover on, but is also encircled by a good variety of other holds. Have the climber do six–eight moves away from this hold, using anything they wish. As soon as the command 'Stop!' is given, the climber must return to the starting hold as swiftly as they can, only using the holds that they have already used.

The climber remains on the starting hold until they are told to start again. They must use different holds each time before returning to their original hold. Repeat this at least four times before changing the start hold.

Beep!

Often a climber's memory skills need working on, particularly those who fail to remember sequences and struggle to pre-read routes or moves.

Set a boulder problem that is between twenty and thirty moves long and is relatively easy for the climber. Leave it unmarked and only point out the holds on the problem to the climber once. Give the climber time to store the information and then have them climb the problem from memory.

When the climber uses or touches an incorrect hold, shout 'Beep!' and point out the correct hold. Tell them to move back one hold before continuing. On their second mistake, they receive another 'Beep!' and must move back two holds, and so on. The climber is not allowed to touch the floor until they complete the problem.

Let them rest and then repeat the problem a few times. The number of 'Beeps' should become smaller.

Variations: Once the climber understands the game, have them commit the footholds to memory as well, to increase the difficulty. If you are going to use this game several times on the same wall, it's worth taking a photo and marking the holds on it, to help remind the person doing the 'Beep' when to 'Beep'.

Un-roped games

109
Count to four

Have you ever watched a person ascend a climb and described their movements as 'jerky'? The climber is probably moving too fast and losing balance during each move.

Set the climber on a problem that is reasonably tricky for them. Each time the climber reaches for a handhold, they must get into a balanced position in order to hold for a count of four. Once the climber has counted to four, they can move their feet. This must be repeated the whole way up the problem.

110
Never-ending journey

Use a hula-hoop and place it on a section of wall. How many laps around it can the climber do? There are a few options available: tell the climber their hands have to go around the outside of the hoop or that the whole body does.

Can the climber do a similar number of laps if they go the other way around? Transfer the hoop to different sections of the wall including overhangs, slabs, vertical sections and those with fewer holds, slopers, big holds, little holds, etc. There are many variables to change and each will make a difference to the number of laps that a climber can do.

111
Setting their own problems

Give the climbers something to mark holds with, e.g. chalk stick or coloured tape, and give them the task of setting their own boulder problems for the rest of the group to try. You could impose all sorts of different rules, depending on what you and they wish to achieve. Rules could include: the person setting the problem must be able to complete it themselves; it must include two slopers; it must have more than six moves; or it has to go in a diagonal direction.

A fun activity for those with a devious mind – setting problems for others.

112
Straight or bent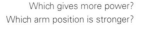

This is an activity to show the relative load bearing strength of using a bent or straight arm when hanging a hold. Find a small hold and have the climber hold it while their same arm is bent at 90 degrees. With the other hand, have them hold their wrist and pull in a downwards direction. Compare this to when they are holding the same hold, but their arm is straight. Is there a difference?

If you hang with a straight arm, you are using very little muscle power. When you do it with a bent arm, it is normally easier for you to pull your hand off the hold. This is partly due to using muscle power to keep the arm bent, but also to do with the change in body position. With a straight arm you are twisted into the wall, while with a bent arm you are normally face on, so the arm is in a position coming away from the wall. When you consider how the climber's centre of mass acts, it doesn't take much to realise that this will act as a lever.

Which gives more power?
Which arm position is stronger?

113

Lucky draw

The preparation for this could be carried out either with the group or before they arrive. Write down all the different climbing moves or holds that you can think of (e.g. layback, pinch, dyno, etc.) including the different names used to describe the same type of move (e.g. bridge and stem). Cut them out and put them into a hat.

With the group, get individuals to select a move at random from the hat. The group much watch the climber performing the move and guess what it is.

Variation: With a climber on the wall, the group have to instruct the climber in the move that they have selected (without saying the actual name of the move). Alternatively, each person selects three moves or hold types at random to incorporate into their own boulder problem.

Fun activities

It is often useful to have a few activities in the back of your mind for when you are climbing with young or particularly nervous people. Games can also be useful when climbing is being used to deliver other important life skills.

114
Teddy bear

Sometimes all you need is an obvious target for the young climber to head for. Chocolate or sweets tend to work but not all parents are happy with their children having teeth-rotting treats. Find that old teddy bear and place at the location you want your students to climb towards.

Having their favourite teddy to climb towards is often just the sort of encouragement that a young climber needs.

115
Jigsaw puzzle

Hide the pieces of a jigsaw puzzle around the wall. Have the group climb around searching for the pieces, which they then have to assemble. You could have the group split into two with two different jigsaws spread over the wall, just to confuse matters.

Variation: Instead of jigsaw pieces, you could have letters that the group can use to form climbing-related words or even clues that would allow them to solve mysteries about their next activity.

116
Spider figures

A group of young climbers have to reproduce prepared figures on the climbing wall using wool, as if they are spiders.

You could have a whole range of rules depending on the ability and experience of the group, as well as the session's aims. These could include, for example, that they all need to be on the wall at the same time or that the whole group must be touching the wool.

This is a great activity to promote teamwork and communication, as well as the climbing-specific aims of body positioning and resting.

117

The artist

Position a piece of A3 paper with the outline of a head drawn on it and a marker pen attached to string near the top of a section of wall. Have the young climbers ascend the wall and draw one feature on the face. In order to draw, they will need to get into a nice, balanced, resting position.

Variation: Have an image made up of straight lines at the foot of the wall. The climbers have to take it in turns to choose a line and then remember it while climbing the wall, before drawing it on the blank sheet of paper at the top.

A distraction is often all that is required to help a climber think about their resting position.

118

On-the-wall spelling 🐾

Write the letters of the alphabet on a card and position them around the bouldering wall. Write down a selection of climbing-related words (equipment, crags, etc.). The young climber selects a word at random and has to climb up and touch all of the letters for that word in the correct order, before climbing back down.

The climber's endurance is likely to get a better work out if they are spelling longer words, but the real aim here is for the climber to look at the wall before getting on it and plan where they need to go. This activity may even provide opportunities for additional relevant teaching, depending on the words that you have selected.

Variation: The group have to guess the word that the climber is spelling, before the climber finishes. By putting the digits 0 to 9 on the wall, the climber could have to give the answer to sums that are written on the paper instead.

119

Three or more legs

Attach a pair of climbers together at the ankle with a piece of bungee cord. Can they traverse a section of the wall while working together? They will have to show elements of teamwork and communication in order to complete this task. This could be used as an exercise to find suitable resting points and will certainly develop the climber's endurance.

Variation: Could you get more people involved? Remember that the first person may have to hang on the wall for a long time before the last person is off the ground.

Roped games

Many of the games described in the other chapters are suitable for use when climbing with ropes, particularly while bottom-roping. Those belaying must be supervised, if appropriate.

Two left, two right

Position a rope so that it hangs down a climb roughly in the middle of the holds for a particular route. The rope is used as a marker to limit how the climber can use their limbs. It could be that they have two limbs to the left of the rope and two to the right. Challenge the climber. Can they still climb the route with one limb on the left and three on the right?

Variation: By hanging two ropes approximately shoulder-width apart, or placing two taped lines down the route, have the climber only use handholds within the lines footholds outside of the lines. This will get the climber really looking for footholds.

Laps on routes

Attempt to climb up and down routes, moving constantly, for a period of 10 minutes. A route that is just over vertical would be the best choice as it would be harder to find rests. The climber will get pumped, but this activity is intended to build endurance. The belayer shouldn't take any of the climber's weight on the rope.

122

No shake, no take

This is an endurance game that can be played while leading or bottom-roping. It requires a route that the climber can only just manage when fresh, that is continuous and without any particular crux sections.

At the start of session when the climber is fresh, they must keep going and are not allowed to shake out or request that the rope be taken in. They must either do all of the moves or fall trying.

At the end of the session, the climber returns to their starting route and climbs it in the same manner, three times. After the first fall, the climber is allowed a minute's rest before trying again. After the second fall, another minute's rest is allowed before the final attempt. The height that the climber reaches on each attempt will probably be decreasing but they must still keep fighting and really push to get to the top. If the climber manages to complete the route each time, then it is too easy for them and they must be set something more challenging next time.

123

Clipping on the ground

Fumbled clipping of quickdraws often leads to wasted energy and possibly even panic setting in. The more efficiently that a climber can clip the rope into quickdraws with either hand and with gates facing in either direction, the better it would be in the long term.

As a warm-up, have the climber clip quickdraws from their harness onto a range of bolts that can be reached from the floor. Get them to use either hand, so that they realise this is a skill for which they need to be ambidextrous.

Set up a quickdraw attached to the wall with the gate facing to the right. Have the climber tie into their harness as normal, using a short piece of rope. While they are standing on the ground, get them to clip the quickdraw with their right hand until they are clipping effectively. Ensure they do not drop the rope or take longer than a few seconds to get the rope into the clip. The climber must watch the rope until it is seated into the karabiner and the gate is shut.

Without changing their technique, reverse the quickdraw so that the gate is facing the opposite direction. Get them to clip this with their right hand, until the skill has been mastered. Now repeat with the process with the left hand, clipping the gate in either direction.

Remember to practise using both hands and with the gate facing both directions.

Clipping on the wall 🤸 ⓧ z^z 🤾 🏃

This is basically the same exercise as clipping on the ground but this time the climber is stationary on the wall. They must focus on getting into a good stable resting position, straight arms and shoulders relaxed, to clip the quickdraw first-go at the first attempt with either hand and with the gate facing either direction.

This works best if the length of rope is very short, so that it can be pulled through the quickdraw each time instead of un-clipping it. Vary the position of the bolt so that the climber is not always clipping in an easy place or off the best holds.

125

A breath with every clip

For some people, the act of clipping the quickdraws will be physically and psychologically the hardest point on any route. This is often caused by them holding their breath before and during the act of clipping. By getting them to relax, they will find things much easier.

Each time the climber gets to an ideal clipping position (the quickdraw level with the body somewhere between the shoulder and the waist), get them to look down, close their eyes, inhale deeply and then exhale before picking up the rope.

This act will reduce the amount of tension in the climber and result in a more relaxing clip. This needs to be practised on every clip.

Learn to relax when leading. It will
make the act of clipping less frantic.

126
Watch the draw

Place quickdraws along the length of a traverse, about 2–3m apart. The climber ties on to a short piece of rope (6m should be plenty) and traverses the wall in both directions, concentrating on clipping the rope in.

When the climber gets to a position that they wish to clip from, get them to keep their eyes on the quickdraw the entire time. If they take their eyes from the draw, they are likely to waste energy fumbling the clip.

As they do this exercise, make sure that the climber varies their clipping position so that they are clipping with both hands and that the quickdraw faces different directions.

You need to ensure that the climber doesn't back-clip, have the rope running behind a leg, or put the rope in their mouth while trying to make the clip.

Variation: Use a longer length of rope to increase rope-drag. Use different traverses of varying steepness to allow this method to be used with a mixed ability group.

An option to practise the skills of leading, but without a belayer.

127

Leading but not

I have often had climbers bottom-roping who find the climbing relatively easy and throw themselves into each new activity at an incredible rate. However, over-enthusiasm can mean that any recently-acquired information regarding body position, or footwork, goes right out window.

To slow them down and to encourage them to focus more carefully, explain the principles of leading. Give them a rope to drag up behind them, while still bottom-roped, and let them have a go at 'leading'. They will often find the act of climbing a bit more challenging and have come back to ask questions.

This is a task that can be used to look at resting, body positioning, effective ways of clipping, endurance and route reading.

Variation: Have a third person, belaying the 'lead' rope. With more instructions, this method is frequently used to directly teach the skills of leading.

With the second rope protecting the climber, they can focus on getting on with the act of clipping in the lead rope.

Index of games

Further reading

Alien Rock Kids Club Toolkit, Johannes Felter, 2005

Betty and the Silver Spider, Craig Luebben, Sharp End Publishing, 2002, ISBN 1-892540-22-3

Climbing Games, Dave Binney and Guido Köstermeyer, British Mountaineering Council

Climbing Rock classic climbs essential skills, British Mountaineering Council, 1998.

Climbing Wall Directory '08, British Mountaineering Council, 2008

Coaching Climbing, Michelle Hurni, The Globe Pequot Press, 2003, ISBN 0-7627-2534-6

Jeux en Escalade, Yves Beroujon, Christophe Gachet, Michel Matera, Pascale Matera, Gilles Mazard and Christian Pruneau, Association prise de tête (Rhône), 1997

Rock climbing essential skills and techniques, Libby Peter, Mountain Leader Training UK, 2004, ISBN 0-9541511-1-9

Rock Climbing for Instructors, Alun Richardson, The Crowood Press, 2001, ISBN 1-86126-422-4

Sport Climbing+, Adrian Berry and Steve McClure, Rockfax Ltd, 2006, ISBN 978-1-873341-86-5

Training Manual for Competition Climbers, Michael Doyle

How to Climb Harder, Mark Reeves, Pesda Press. 2009, ISBN 978-1-906095-11-6